This book is dedicated to weirdos who are intrigued by dark and disturbing things.

This coloring book is imbued with Source protection to keep you from
picking up unpleasant attachments while in coloring deep-trance.
It is your responsibility to hold this intention of protection while in use.

If you're a dumbass and you're looking to by-pass this protection
simply scribble out the words below.

I AM UNDER PROTECTION WHILE USING THIS BOOK

Enjoy these coloring pages.
Please leave a review on Amazon
and share your ideas for future coloring books.

this page intentionally left blank

this page intentionally left blank

DENNIS RAIDER

03/09/1945
PITTSBURG
KANSAS

CUB SCOUTS

JOHN SANDFORD
RULES
OF PREY

never kill anyone
...you know

BTK
KILLER

K·SCHROEDER '17

this page intentionally left blank

this page intentionally left blank

this page intentionally left blank

Dorothea Puente
January.9-1929-March.27.2011
Redlands, CA

Sominex SLEEP AID 32 TABLETS

DEATH HOUSE LANDLADY

this page intentionally left blank

The Red Ripper
Andrei Chikatilo

16 October 1936
14 February 1994
Yabluchne, Ukrainian SSR

this page intentionally left blank

JERRY BRUDOS

WEBSTER
SOUTH
DAKOTA
01/31/1939
03/28/2006

this page intentionally left blank

this page intentionally left blank

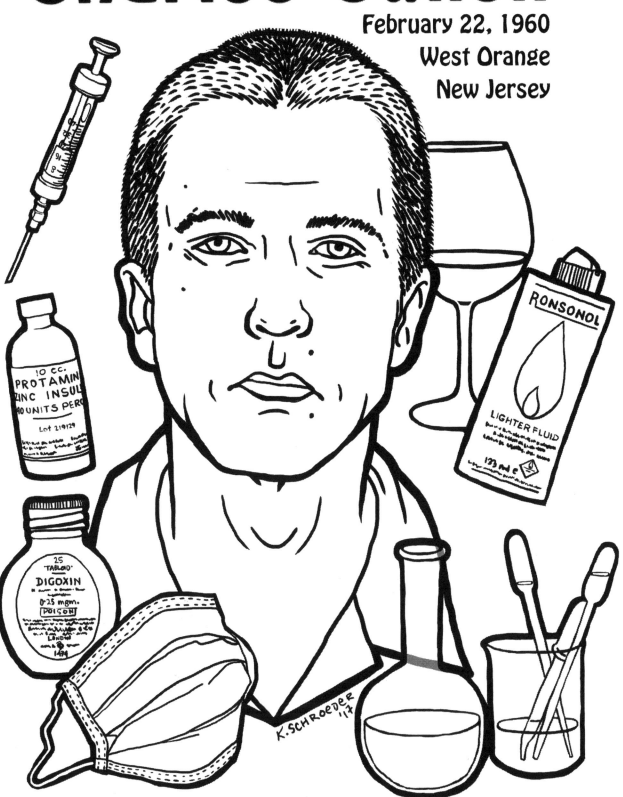

Henry Lee Lucas

Aug 23, 1936
Mar 12, 2001
Blacksburg,
Virginia

K. SCHROEDER '17

this page intentionally left blank

Quite!

Julie
James
Molly
Erik
Noah

K.SCHROEDER '17

Waneta Hoyt - Richford NY
5-13 1946 to 8-13 1998

this page intentionally left blank

this page intentionally left blank

this page intentionally left blank

Anna Marie Hahn

July 7, 1906
Bavaria,
Germany

Arsenic Anna
Blonde Borgia
Angel of Mercy

OHIO DERBY
5 FIVE DOLLARS 5
OH DERBY
NO 7 SEVEN
EIGHTH (8) RACE
WIN
4 MAY 1932

K. SCHROEDER '16

POISON
GRANULES
OF
ARSENIC
1.50 Grai nea.

TED BUNDY
NOV 24, 1946 - JAN 24, 1989

BURLINGTON, VERMONT

this page intentionally left blank

this page intentionally left blank

Mary Flora Bell
The Tyneside Strangler

26 May 1957 - Newcastle upon Tyne, England - Released

K. SCHROEDER '17

this page intentionally left blank

this page intentionally left blank

ED KEMPER

DECEMBER 18, 1948

BURBANK
CALIFORNIA

THE
CO-ED
BUTCHER

K. SCHROEDER '17

this page intentionally left blank

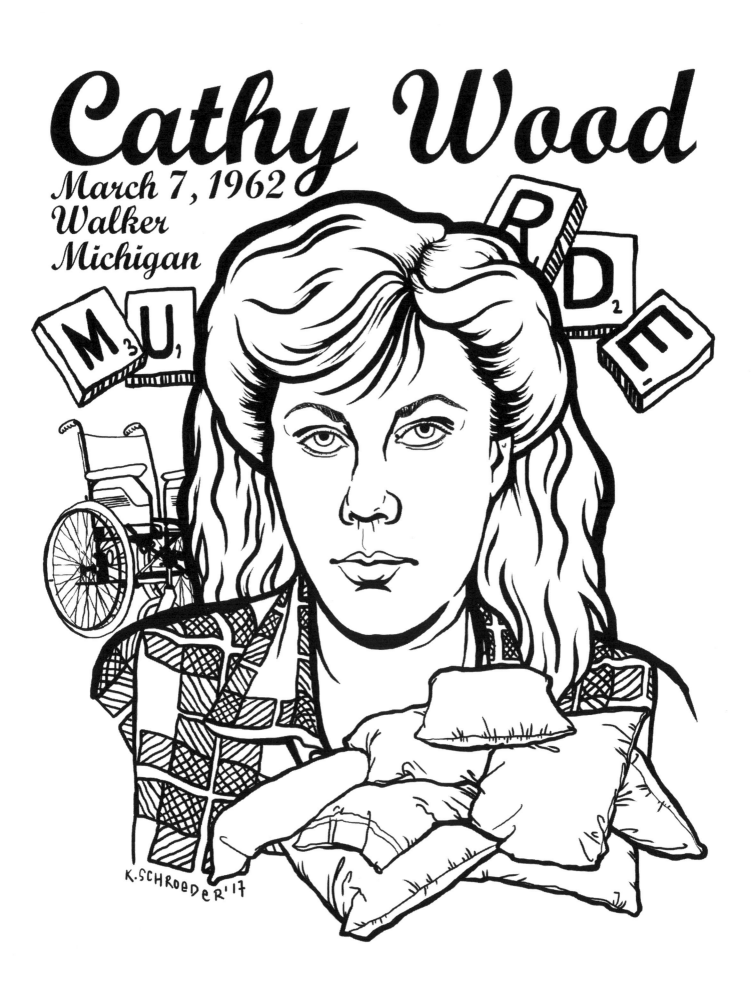

Cathy Wood

March 7, 1962
Walker
Michigan

K. SCHROEDER '17

this page intentionally left blank

Edward Theodore Gein

8/27 1906
7/26 1984

Wisconsin

The
Mad
Butcher

this page intentionally left blank

Donald Henry Gaskin

03/13/1933
09/06/1991
Florence, SC

K. SCHROEDER '17

WELCOME TO
SOUTH CAROLINA
SAFE DRIVING
SAVES LIVES

Hitchikers' Killer

this page intentionally left blank

this page intentionally left blank

zodiak killer
identity unknown

San Francisco 12/1968 - 10/1969

this page intentionally left blank

this page intentionally left blank

this page intentionally left blank

this page intentionally left blank

Alexander Pichuskin
Chessboard Killer

Moscow, Russia   April 9, 1974

K. SCHROEDER '17

Life is cheaper than sausage

this page intentionally left blank

Robert Berdella

Kansas City Butcher

Cuyahoga Falls, Ohio
January 31, 1949
October 8, 1992

bob's bazaar bizarre

POLAROID

K. SCHRIEDER 2014

this page intentionally left blank

Lizzie Borden

July 19, 1860

Fall River, Ma.

K SCHROEDER '16

this page intentionally left blank

this page intentionally left blank

this page intentionally left blank

TEST OUT COLORS

this page intentionally left blank

Made in the USA
San Bernardino, CA
02 November 2018